AF270422

NEW YORK METS

BY DAVID J. CLARKE

SportsZone

An Imprint of Abdo Publishing
abdobooks.com

abdobooks.com

Published by Abdo Publishing, a division of ABDO, PO Box 398166, Minneapolis, Minnesota 55439. Copyright © 2023 by Abdo Consulting Group, Inc. International copyrights reserved in all countries. No part of this book may be reproduced in any form without written permission from the publisher. SportsZone™ is a trademark and logo of Abdo Publishing.

Printed in China.
102022
012023

Cover Photo: Jim McIsaac/Getty Images Sport/Getty Images
Interior Photos: Daniel Shirey/MLB Photos/Getty Images, 4, 6, 21; Blank Archives/Hulton Archive/Getty Images, 8; Bettmann/Getty Images, 9; AP Images, 10; Focus on Sport/Getty Images, 12, 15, 16, 20, 26, 28; Louis Requena/Sporting News/Getty Images, 18; Paul J. Bereswill/Newsday RM/Getty Images, 22; Ron Vesely/MLB Photos/Getty Images Sport/Getty Images, 25; Ronald C. Modra/Getty Images Sport/Getty Images, 29; Paul Benoit/AP Images, 30; David Seelig/Getty Images Sport/Getty Images, 32; Matt Campbell/AFP/Getty Images, 34; Al Bello/Getty Images Sport/Getty Images, 37; David Maxwell/Getty Images Sport/Getty Images, 38; Mike Stobe/Getty Images Sport/Getty Images, 39; Justin Edmonds/Getty Images Sport/Getty Images, 41

Editor: Steph Giedd
Series Designer: Becky Daum

Library of Congress Control Number: 2022940485

Publisher's Cataloging-in-Publication Data

Names: Clarke, David J., author.
Title: New York Mets / by David J. Clarke
Description: Minneapolis, Minnesota: Abdo Publishing, 2023 | Series: Inside MLB | Includes online resources and index.
Identifiers: ISBN 9781098290252 (lib. bdg.) | ISBN 9781098275457 (ebook)
Subjects: LCSH: New York Mets (Baseball team)--Juvenile literature. | Baseball teams--Juvenile literature. | Professional sports--Juvenile literature. | Sports franchises--Juvenile literature. | Major League Baseball (Organization)--Juvenile literature.
Classification: DDC 796.35764--dc23

CONTENTS

MEET THE METS

The 37-year-old pitcher leaned in to take the sign from New York Mets catcher Tomás Nido. Max Scherzer had San Francisco Giants center fielder Steven Duggar in the hole at 0–2. Scherzer had already thrown 101 pitches. The righty knew his next toss could be his last of the night.

The fans at New York's Citi Field knew it too. They rose from their seats to urge on their new ace. Mets supporters knew they had a contending team entering the 2022 season. That was especially true after general manager Billy Eppler shelled out $130 million over three years to bring Scherzer in as a free agent that off-season. The three-time Cy Young Award winner had been one of baseball's best pitchers for more than

Max Scherzer pitches during his first home game with the Mets on April 19, 2022.

Scherzer was a three-time Cy Young Award winner prior to his first season with the Mets in 2022.

a decade. Now, on April 19, 2022, he was making his Mets home debut.

It had already been a good day at Citi Field. The Mets won the first game of a doubleheader in walk-off fashion to defeat the Giants 5–4. In the nightcap, Scherzer was taking down Giant after Giant. Through 6 2/3 innings, he had nine strikeouts.

Nido signaled for a changeup. Often when a pitcher is up 0–2, he will throw something out of the strike zone and hope the batter will chase the pitch. Scherzer and Nido decided not to. Instead, the righty dropped a perfect strike on the outside corner to the left-handed hitter. The crowd erupted as the home plate umpire called Duggar out. The stunned Giants outfielder hung his head as he strolled back to the dugout.

Scherzer walked off the mound to an ovation from his new fans. His work was finished. Two innings later, the Mets had their doubleheader sweep, and New York had a new hero.

A REPLACEMENT TEAM

In the late 1950s, New York baseball fans weren't looking for a hero so much as a team. Through the 1957 season, New York had been home to three Major League Baseball (MLB) clubs. The New York Yankees were the most successful team in history. The American League (AL) powerhouse had won 19 World Series titles through 1961.

However, the city also had two National League (NL) teams. The New York Giants and Brooklyn Dodgers were among the league's most historic franchises. The rivalry was intense between the two beloved teams. But in 1958, both teams suddenly left town. The Dodgers moved to Los Angeles, and the Giants left for San Francisco.

The wait for a new NL team did not last long. MLB was expanding in the early 1960s. And lawyer William Shea suggested a new team for New York. Originally, they were to play in the Continental League, a new league Shea was helping

The 1962 Mets played at the Polo Grounds. Shea Stadium, shown on the Mets program, would be their new home in 1964.

to start. But an agreement was reached for the new league not to compete with MLB. Instead, four teams, two from the Continental League, would join the established league. The new club in New York would start playing in the NL in 1962.

The team called back to New York's baseball past for both its nickname and uniform colors. They used the nickname "Metropolitans" after a team from the 1880s. Newspaper writers knew that wouldn't fit on a headline, so it was quickly shortened to Mets. When the players took the field, they were wearing white, orange, and blue uniforms. The orange was a nod to the Giants, while the blue was famously a Dodgers color. The team also played its first two seasons in the Giants' old stadium, the Polo Grounds in the borough of Manhattan.

Mets manager Casey Stengel waves to the crowd at what was supposed to be the opening game of the 1962 season, but the game was rained out.

THE AMAZIN' METS

Even the team's first manager was a throwback to New York's baseball past. Casey Stengel had played for both the Giants and the Dodgers in the 1910s and 1920s. He then managed the Dodgers in the 1930s before going on to enormous success with the Yankees. From 1949 to 1958, Stengel managed the AL team to seven World Series titles.

With the Yankees, Stengel had some of baseball's best players. The same could not be said of the Mets. During spring training, Stengel tried to rally support for the team by telling fans, "Come and see my 'Amazin' Mets'!" The nickname stuck, but the Mets were amazing for all the wrong reasons.

First baseman "Marvelous" Marv Throneberry reaches for a wild throw during a 1962 game.

The original team was a mix of cast-offs and older players whose talents were fading. Even a brilliant manager like Stengel couldn't save them. The Mets' first season was one of the worst MLB had ever seen. New York hit an NL-worst .240. Its team earned-run average (ERA) was 5.04, by far the worst in the league. It all added up to a dreadful 40–120 record. But numbers told only half the story. The 1962 Mets lost in remarkable fashion.

The Mets' starting infield of first baseman "Marvelous" Marv Throneberry, second baseman Charlie Neal, shortstop Elio Chacón, and third baseman Félix Mantilla made a combined 87 errors. Utilityman Rod Kanehl added 32 more. Players crashed into each other in the outfield chasing pop flies. Catchers botched easy pitches. Stengel said of his team, "I've been in this game 100 years, but I see new ways to lose 'em I never knew existed before."

Despite their terrible play, NL fans who missed baseball embraced the Mets. The team didn't win more than 53 games in its first four years, but it drew around 1 million fans each season. That number jumped closer to 2 million after the team opened its new ballpark, Shea Stadium, in Queens in 1964.

Stengel left the team in 1965. The Mets did not improve under new manager Wes Westrum. Through the 1967 season, New York never finished better than 66–95. But the Mets were about to put together one of the most memorable turnarounds in baseball history.

CHAPTER 2

THE MIRACLE METS

Going into the 1968 season, the Mets hired a new manager. Like Casey Stengel, Gil Hodges was a New York baseball legend. The former Brooklyn Dodgers first baseman was well respected by his players. He was a fair, steady leader who became known as a great teacher.

However, it didn't really show in his first season. The Mets finished ninth in the 10-team NL, 24 games out of first. While the team was still bad, it was the first time New York had cracked 70 wins.

No one expected much from the Mets as they opened play in 1969. And the team promptly started the year by losing seven of its first 10 games. But these were not the same Mets.

Ace Tom Seaver was the 1967 Rookie of the Year for the Mets. He went on to become a three-time Cy Young Award winner as the best pitcher in the NL.

The rest of the NL started to figure that out when New York turned things around and sat 53–39 at the All-Star break in July.

PITCHING A WINNER

The 1969 Mets didn't have a great offense. Left fielder Cleon Jones was third in the NL with a .340 average. But only one other Met, part-time starter Art Shamsky, even hit. 300. Center fielder Tommie Agee was the team's only 20-home-run hitter. Only three teams in the NL scored fewer runs than New York.

The reason the 1969 Mets won games was a tremendous pitching staff. The group got used to winning low-scoring games. Lefty Jerry Koosman finished 17–9 despite missing time early in the season. Rookie Gary Gentry won 13 games. Ron Taylor, Tug McGraw, and Nolan Ryan, just 22 years old, were reliable members of Hodges's pitching staff.

The ace of the staff was 24-year-old Tom Seaver. The Mets were lucky to have Seaver

YOUNG RYAN

Nolan Ryan was just 22 in 1969, his third season with the team. He appeared in only 25 games that year for the Mets. But it was just the start of an amazing 27-year career. After two more years as a part-time starter for the Mets, he was traded to the California Angels. Until he retired in 1993, Ryan rode his intimidating "Ryan Express" fastball to MLB records of 5,714 strikeouts and seven no-hitters. He played for four teams, including the Houston Astros and Texas Rangers, but he never made the World Series again.

at all. In 1966 the Atlanta Braves drafted him. At the time, Seaver was pitching for the University of Southern California (USC). The Braves offered him a contract after USC's season began, a violation of MLB rules. Atlanta was forced to give Seaver up, and the Mets won his rights in a special lottery.

In 1969 Seaver won the NL Cy Young Award as the league's best pitcher. He started 35 games and finished 18 of them. His 25 wins led the league. The righty was known as a technician with perfect mechanics and great accuracy. After Seaver eventually left the Mets in 1977, his new manager Sparky Anderson once said of him, "My idea of managing is giving the ball to Tom Seaver and sitting down and watching him work."

The 1969 season was the first time MLB divided the AL and NL up into two divisions each. That year also saw the

Hall of Fame pitcher Nolan Ryan played the first five of his 27 seasons with the Mets.

Jerry Koosman prepares to deliver a pitch during the 1969 World Series.

postseason expand to allow two teams from each league. The Mets were in the NL East. Despite their great season, the Mets still trailed the division-leading Chicago Cubs by 10 games in

August. But New York caught fire, passed the Cubs, and won the division by eight games with a 100–62 record. Then the Mets swept Atlanta 3–0 in the first ever NL Championship Series (NLCS).

SHOE POLISH

In the World Series, the Mets faced the Baltimore Orioles, who had won 109 games. Baltimore was a heavy favorite, and no one was surprised when the Orioles took the first game 4–1.

However, the Mets rallied back in Game 2, winning 2–1 behind Koosman and Taylor. Gentry and Ryan then shut out Baltimore 5–0 in Game 3 at Shea Stadium, backed by two excellent outfield plays by Agee. The Mets won Game 4 on a walk-off play in the 10th inning when the Orioles made an error on a sacrifice bunt. Suddenly the Mets had a chance to clinch a championship at home.

The Orioles jumped out to a 3–0 lead in Game 5. But everything changed in the bottom of the sixth, thanks to the eagle eye of Hodges. Jones led off the inning and appeared to be hit in the foot by a low pitch from Baltimore's Dave McNally. Hodges showed home plate umpire Lou DiMuro a tiny spot of shoe polish on the ball, proving that the ball had hit Jones's foot. Jones was awarded first base. The next batter was veteran Donn Clendenon, who homered over the left-field wall.

Following a legendary playing career, Yogi Berra took over as the Mets' manager in 1972.

In the seventh, second baseman Al Weis hit a home run to tie it up. The Mets then surged ahead on right fielder Ron Swoboda's double in the eighth, which scored one run. It was 5–3 in the ninth when Koosman came back out. He walked the leadoff batter, then got the next three batters out. After seven years as laughingstocks, the Mets were suddenly champions. The players celebrated by racing for the dugout. Right behind them were jubilant fans who proceeded to tear up Shea Stadium's turf to take home with them.

YA GOTTA BELIEVE

In 1972 Hodges unexpectedly died after suffering a heart attack. In his place came another baseball legend, Yogi Berra. A former star catcher for the New York Yankees under Stengel, Berra was also famous for his quotes.

In 1973 the Mets were last in the NL East at the end of July. A reporter asked Berra for his thoughts. The manager reportedly delivered one of his most famous sayings: "It ain't over 'til it's over." No one knows if Berra said those exact words. But the Mets played the rest of the season as if he had. The Mets rallied past their five division rivals to win the NL East with an 82–79 record.

One saying that was certainly true came from McGraw, the team's stud reliever. During a team meeting in July, the

excitable McGraw shouted at his teammates, "Ya gotta believe!" It became the team's rallying cry that year, and the phrase is still used by Mets fans today.

That mantra took the Mets through the NLCS and into the World Series against the Oakland Athletics. But New York's luck ran out there. Leading the series 3–2, the Mets stumbled in the last two games of a seven-game defeat.

THE MIDNIGHT MASSACRE

Seaver was the Cy Young winner again in 1973. And over the next three seasons, he remained one of the league's best pitchers. He won the award again in 1975. In 1976 Seaver led the NL in strikeouts for the fifth time in seven years.

Even better, Seaver became the ultimate baseball hero for Mets fans. "Tom Terrific" was by far the best player the

Seaver's impact on the Mets was so great that the team now has a statue of his likeness outside of their stadium, Citi Field.

team had ever had. But Seaver did not get along with team chairman M. Donald Grant. The two fought over the contract renegotiations. After they failed to reach an agreement, the Mets decided to trade the star pitcher. On the night of June 15, 1977, Seaver was dealt to the Cincinnati Reds. Upset Mets fans called the trade "the Midnight Massacre."

It certainly destroyed the team on the field. Without its ace, the Mets stumbled to 98 losses. It was New York's worst season since 1967. And it would be a while before things got better again.

CHAPTER 3

"A MILLION WORDS"

n 1980 the Mets were on their way to a fourth-straight season with 90 losses. It was a bad year on the field, but it turned out to be a huge turning point for the team.

Earlier that year, the team's new owners, Fred Wilpon and Nelson Doubleday Jr., hired Frank Cashen as general manager. Cashen was a sharp baseball mind who had helped build the 1969 Baltimore Orioles team the Mets had beaten in the World Series. He got to work right away rebuilding his new club.

Cashen started collecting talent wherever he could. Outfielder Darryl Strawberry was the team's top draft pick in 1980. Fellow outfielder Mookie Wilson was already in the Mets'

Slugger Darryl Strawberry cheers as his three-run homer sails over the fence in 1986. He also won the Home Run Derby that season.

farm system. Rugged center fielder Lenny Dykstra was picked in 1981. Phenom pitcher Dwight Gooden was drafted in 1982.

Some trades netted the Mets catcher Gary Carter, starting pitcher Ron Darling, third baseman Ray Knight, and first baseman Keith Hernandez. New York had a well-rounded team.

LET'S GO METS

In 1985 the Mets came just short of the playoffs. But they had all the pieces in place. Strawberry was emerging as a superstar. Gooden won the Cy Young Award at age 20 with an incredible season. He went 24–4 with a 1.53 ERA. Many wondered if he could be baseball's best pitcher ever.

In addition, Hernandez and Carter offered veteran leadership along with All-Star play. As 1986 opened, the Mets looked unbeatable. They also had swagger and style. The 1986 Mets were loud and brash. Darling described the team as a "traveling rock show." They stayed out late, but they still showed up to the ballpark ready to win. Manager Davey Johnson didn't mind what they did off the field if the results were there. The approach worked. The 1986 Mets won 108 games, a team record.

Even that dominant record didn't mean the playoffs would be easy. The Mets split the first four games of the NLCS against

Ace Dwight Gooden led the majors in strikeouts during his first two seasons with the Mets in 1984 and 1985.

the Houston Astros. Only a walk-off home run by Dykstra in Game 3 kept New York from a 3–1 hole.

The Mets needed two more dramatic wins to reach the World Series. Carter's 12th-inning walk-off single won Game 5. Game 6 went to 16 innings in Houston. The Mets finally pulled out a 7–6 win in what was the longest postseason game ever at the time.

ANOTHER MIRACLE

The drama of the NLCS had nothing on the World Series. The Mets were paired up with the AL-champion Boston Red Sox,

Gary Carter, *center*, celebrates with teammates after hitting a game-winning RBI single during Game 5 of the 1986 NLCS.

who were looking for their first title since 1918. Boston looked good in winning the first two games in New York. But the Mets rallied to even the series. Boston pitcher Bruce Hurst shut down the Mets in Game 5, and New York faced elimination.

That sent the teams back to Shea Stadium for one of the most memorable World Series games ever. Twice, the Red Sox built leads only for the Mets to rally back. After Carter's sacrifice fly tied the game 3–3 in the eighth, the game eventually went to extra innings.

Boston scored two quick runs off Mets reliever Rick Aguilera in the top of the 10th. That looked like it would be enough after Red Sox pitcher Calvin Schiraldi got the first two outs in the bottom half. Writers in the press box were told Hurst would be World Series Most Valuable Player (MVP). The scoreboard briefly flashed a message that said, "Congratulations Red Sox."

However, there was still one out to go. And none of the Mets hitters wanted to be that out. Carter kept the game alive with a single. After his hit, Carter then told first-base coach Bill Robinson that he wasn't going to be the last out of the World Series. Pinch-hitter Kevin Mitchell repeated the same sentence to Robinson after he singled.

Knight was the next batter. He singled to knock in Carter, and he also told Robinson he didn't want to be the last out. By now Mets fans had started to believe the team could come back. The crowd rose as Boston manager John McNamara replaced Schiraldi with Bob Stanley.

FAN MAN

Adding to the drama of Game 6 of the 1986 World Series was a fan who parachuted onto the field during the top of the first inning. Actor Michael Sergio dropped into the infield holding a sign that read "Go Mets." Security quickly grabbed Sergio. He was led off the field through the Mets dugout, where pitcher Ron Darling gave Sergio a high five as the intruder was taken down the clubhouse tunnel.

Ray Knight (22) arrives at home plate to score the winning run in the bottom of the 10th inning in Game 6 of the 1986 World Series.

Wilson was the next hitter for the Mets, with Mitchell at third and Knight at first. Wilson proceeded to foul off pitch after pitch from Stanley. The right-hander's 2–2 pitch came down and in to Wilson, who was batting left-handed, and skipped to the backstop. Mitchell sprinted home, and the game was tied.

Knight had moved to second base on the wild pitch. Wilson could now win the game with a single. But he managed only a chopper up the first-base line. Waiting there was Boston first baseman, 36-year-old Bill Buckner. The veteran had aching ankles and couldn't get down to play the last hop. As the ball rolled into right field, Knight came around to score the improbable winning run.

The stadium erupted. Players on both teams looked shocked at what they had just seen. On television, announcers Vin Scully and Joe Garagiola stayed silent for more than three minutes to allow viewers to soak in the images of the celebrating Mets and the stunned Red Sox. Finally, the legendary play-by-play man Scully summed up the moment. "If one picture is worth a thousand words, you have seen about a million words . . ." Scully said. "The Mets are not only alive, but they are well, and

Mets center fielder Mookie Wilson hit .269 but also had six strikeouts during the 1986 World Series.

Mets catcher Gary Carter leaps into the arms of relief pitcher Jesse Orosco after their Game 7 victory to win the 1986 World Series.

they will play the Red Sox in Game 7 tomorrow." However, due to a rainout, they played two nights later.

The Mets rallied again to win the final game. After falling behind 3–0, they scored six straight runs in an eventual 8–5 victory. But it was the amazing finish to Game 6 that was the lasting memory of New York's championship season.

COLLAPSE

No one in baseball thought the 1986 championship would be the last for that group of Mets. But the core didn't stay together long. Cashen let Knight go just six weeks after the 1986 season was over.

The saddest fall for the 1986 team came from both Strawberry and Gooden. The two young stars both struggled with drug and alcohol problems. They both eventually recovered and played long careers. However, they were never as great as when they were young stars with the Mets.

Even with those struggles, the Mets reached the playoffs in 1988. There the Los Angeles Dodgers upset them. Hernandez, Dykstra, Wilson, and Carter were all gone from New York by 1990. Cashen left his job after the Mets finished 77–84 in 1991.

The front office tried to rebuild the Mets quickly by signing high-priced free agents over the next few years. None worked out. New York spent millions only to lose 103 games in 1993. Less than a decade after having the greatest team in club history, the Mets were a mess.

ANTHONY YOUNG

Pitcher Anthony Young began the 1993 season by losing his first 13 decisions. He had also lost his last 14 decisions of 1992. The 27-game losing streak set an MLB record. Young finally got a win to end the drought on July 28, 1993. He wasn't all bad during that stretch. Young did record 12 saves and even had a streak of 23 2/3 scoreless innings as a reliever.

CHAPTER 4

SEARCHING FOR STARS

Mets general manager Steve Phillips already had several talented players on the roster when he was promoted to the general manager spot in July 1997. First baseman John Olerud was a former batting champion and two-time World Series winner with the Toronto Blue Jays. Slick-fielding shortstop Rey Ordóñez and hard-hitting third baseman Edgardo Alfonzo were two young stars. Veteran reliever John Franco had been with the team since 1990. The Brooklyn native was a hometown favorite.

Phillips went out and started adding big names to put the team over the top. He traded for lefty Al Leiter before the 1998 season. During that same year, Phillips added slugging

Catcher Mike Piazza hit 220 home runs in his eight seasons with the Mets.

catcher Mike Piazza, who was one of the best power hitters in the league. Before the 1999 season, Phillips added star third baseman Robin Ventura. Alfonzo moved to second base to give the Mets a dynamic infield.

SUBWAY SERIES

Those pieces got New York back to the playoffs in 1999. The Mets came up short in a thrilling 4–2 NLCS loss to the Atlanta Braves. Of the six games, five were decided by one run.

In 2000 the Mets were ready to contend again. Olerud had left the team, but Phillips added more strong pitching by trading for lefty Mike Hampton. Led by manager Bobby Valentine and Piazza's 38 home runs, the Mets slugged their way to the World Series.

In the 1940s and 1950s, New York had four teams: the New York Yankees, Giants, and Mets, as well as the Brooklyn Dodgers. World Series matchups between these teams at the time became known

Robin Ventura won his sixth and final Gold Glove as the league's top fielding third baseman in 1999, his first year with the Mets.

as the "Subway Series." Since the Dodgers and Giants moved their teams to California, the Mets could not make the Series happen again.

The Mets and the Yankees had always fought for New York fans. But they had never met on the field until interleague play started in 1997, allowing NL and AL teams to play during the season. Three years later, when the Mets rolled through the two rounds of the playoffs, they found the Yankees waiting for them.

By 2000 the rivalry had heated up between the Mets and the Yankees. It got worse that summer. In July Yankees pitcher Roger Clemens had hit Piazza in the head with a fastball. Most observers thought Clemens hit Piazza intentionally. The slugger had already hit three home runs in 12 at-bats against Clemens over his career.

All eyes were on the pair again in the top of the first inning in Game 2 of the World Series. Piazza fouled off a Clemens pitch. The ball rolled wide of first, but Piazza's bat broke in half.

The barrel went straight to Clemens, who grabbed it and threw it back at Piazza's feet.

Piazza later hit a home run in the ninth inning as the Mets tried to rally from a 6–0 hole. They came up short as the Yankees held on for a 6–5 win and a 2–0 series lead. The Mets won Game 3 at home but lost two more close decisions in Games 4 and 5. The Mets watched the Yankees celebrate a championship on Shea Stadium turf.

REYES AND WRIGHT

More free agents came in to try to keep the Mets in contention in the early 2000s. But New York's top stars once again came from their own farm system. Shortstop José Reyes debuted in 2003, and third baseman David Wright debuted in 2004. Within three years, they were the heartbeat of the team. They also nearly brought the Mets back to the World Series.

In 2006 both Wright and Reyes hit over .300. Veteran first baseman Carlos Delgado hit 38 home runs. And center fielder Carlos Beltrán hit a team-high 41 to round out an exceptional offense. A veteran pitching staff paced the Mets to the NLCS against the St. Louis Cardinals. However, New York's World Series dreams fell apart in the top of the ninth inning in Game 7 at Shea Stadium. Cardinals catcher Yadier Molina's two-run homer broke a 1–1 tie and doomed New York to a 3–1 defeat.

Shortstop José Reyes gets the out and turns a double play against the Montreal Expos.

SO LONG, SHEA

Once again the Mets could not maintain excellence. They had winning records in 2007 and 2008 but did not reach the playoffs. The 2008 season was also the final year of Shea Stadium. The Mets' new ballpark, Citi Field, was set to open right next door.

While the park was shiny and new, it lacked the memories of Shea. And it took a while for the Mets to create more. The team finished in fourth place each of Citi Field's first four seasons. In 2015 the Mets finally put a contender on the new diamond.

By then Reyes had left the team. The now 32-year-old Wright was limited to just 38 games by a back injury. Instead, the Mets leaned on a group of young pitchers for success. Righty Jacob deGrom had been the NL Rookie of the Year in 2014. He was joined by 26-year-old Matt Harvey and 22-year-old Noah Syndergaard in the rotation. All three racked up strikeouts as the Mets won the NL East.

The trio was excellent as the Mets outlasted the Los Angeles Dodgers in the division series, then swept the Chicago Cubs

Slugging third baseman David Wright played his entire 14-year career with the Mets.

Ace Jacob deGrom led the NL in strikeouts in 2019 and 2020.

in the NLCS. They also received a historic offensive boost from Daniel Murphy. The second baseman set an MLB postseason record by homering in six consecutive games during the first two rounds.

New York's run ended in the World Series again. This time they lost in five games to the Kansas City Royals. Two of the losses, including the deciding Game 5, came in extra innings.

MODERN METS

Throughout their history, the Mets have never had extended periods of success. The 2015 team was no different. They reached the NL wild-card game in 2016 but plummeted to fourth place a year later. This time injuries were the biggest issue. Harvey and Syndergaard both struggled to stay on the field. DeGrom was still excellent and won the first of two straight Cy Young Awards in 2018. But he could not carry the team alone. And after fan favorite Wright finally retired in 2018, the Mets were also trying to find the next homegrown offensive star.

The wait was short. But the player who arrived in 2019 was a surprise. First baseman Pete Alonso was not expected to make the Mets' roster that year. But after he hit .352 with four home runs in spring training, manager Mickey Calloway named Alonso the starter.

The 6-foot-3-inch, 245-pound slugger proved his spring wasn't just luck as soon as he arrived in New York. He quickly started mashing home runs. On August 18, Alonso hit his 40th to break the NL rookie record.

Next up was the MLB rookie record of 52, set by the Yankees' Aaron Judge just two years earlier. Alonso passed Judge on September 28 with a solo shot at Citi Field against the Atlanta Braves in a 3–0 win.

Pete Alonso celebrates his 2021 Home Run Derby victory. He also won the competition in 2019, his debut season.

It took New York a few years to build on the success of 2019. Entering the 2022 season, the front office knew the Mets could be a contender. General manager Billy Eppler had built a solid offense around Alonso while also adding star pitchers Chris Bassitt and Max Scherzer.

The 2022 Mets won 101 games. That was the team's most since its championship year of 1986. And while the 2022 team fell short of the World Series, Mets fans hoped the team's next championship was just around the corner.

1962

Led by legendary manager Casey Stengel, the Mets make their debut and finish the year just 40–120.

1964

The Mets lose 109 games in their first season playing at Shea Stadium.

1967

Ace Tom Seaver makes his MLB debut with the Mets and is named Rookie of the Year.

1968

New York hires manager Gil Hodges in October of 1967 and finishes above last place for just the second time in team history the following season.

1969

The "Miracle Mets" win 100 games and upset the Baltimore Orioles to win their first World Series.

1973

Spurred on by reliever Tug McGraw's slogan of "Ya gotta believe!" the Mets reach the World Series but lose in seven games to the Oakland Athletics.

1977

The Mets trade fan favorite Tom Seaver in June, a move dubbed "the Midnight Massacre."

1980

After several years of losing, New York hires veteran general manager Frank Cashen. Outfielder Darryl Strawberry is taken with the top pick in the MLB draft.

1985

Dwight Gooden, at just 20 years old, puts together an incredible pitching season. He finishes 24–4 with a 1.53 ERA and wins the NL Cy Young Award.

1986

Spurred on by an incredible three-run comeback in the 10th inning of Game 6, the Mets win the World Series over the Boston Red Sox.

1993

The high-priced Mets lose 103 games, their first 100-loss season since 1967.

1999

Led by catcher Mike Piazza, the Mets return to the playoffs for the first time since 1988.

2000

The Mets lose a "Subway Series" to their crosstown rivals, the New York Yankees, 4–1.

2009

The Mets open their new ballpark, Citi Field.

2015

Led by a trio of young pitchers, the Mets reach the World Series but lose 4–1 to the Kansas City Royals.

2019

First baseman Pete Alonso sets an MLB rookie record with 53 home runs.

TEAM FACTS

FRANCHISE HISTORY

New York Mets (1962–)

WORLD SERIES CHAMPIONSHIPS

1969, 1986

KEY PLAYERS

Pete Alonso (2019–)
Carlos Beltrán (2005–11)
Gary Carter (1985–89)
Ron Darling (1983–91)
Jacob deGrom (2014–)
Lenny Dykstra (1985–89)
Dwight Gooden (1984–94)
Bud Harrelson (1965–77)
Keith Hernandez (1983–89)
Jerry Koosman (1967–78)
Al Leiter (1998–2004)
Mike Piazza (1998–2005)
José Reyes (2003–11, 2016–18)
Tom Seaver (1967–77, 1983)
Darryl Strawberry (1983–90)
Mookie Wilson (1980–89)
David Wright (2004–18)

KEY MANAGERS

Gil Hodges (1968–71)
Davey Johnson (1984–90)
Bobby Valentine (1996–2002)

HOME STADIUMS

Polo Grounds (1962–63)
Shea Stadium (1964–2008)
Citi Field (2009–)

TEAM TRIVIA

THE BEATLES AT SHEA

In August 1965, the Beatles played a 30-minute concert in front of 56,000 fans at Shea Stadium. It was considered the first-ever open-air stadium rock concert.

UNDER .500

From 1962 to 1968, the Mets had a winning record for only two days. The Mets won their third game of the season on April 17, 1966, to improve to 2–1. It was the first time they were ever above .500 at any point in a season. Two days later, they started a five-game losing streak. A winning record didn't happen again until New York started 2–1 in 1969.

SOMEBODY SCORE

On April 15, 1968, the Mets and the Houston Astros played a 1–0 game that took six hours, six minutes to play. The winning run didn't come until Houston's Norm Miller scored on an error by New York shortstop Al Weis with the bases loaded in the bottom of the 24th inning. It was the longest scoreless game in MLB history.

HAPLESS HARRY

One of the stranger 1962 Mets stories was that of catcher Harry Chiti. New York picked him up in a trade with Cleveland for a "player to be named later." That meant New York would send someone to Cleveland later in the season to complete the deal. Chiti played so badly in 15 games for the Mets that they decided to send the catcher back. Chiti became the first MLB player ever to be traded for himself.

GLOSSARY

ace

A team's best starting pitcher.

contender

A person or team that has a good chance at winning a championship.

debut

First appearance.

farm system

In baseball, all the minor league teams that feed players to one major league team.

free agent

A player whose rights are not owned by any team.

general manager

An executive who runs a team and is responsible for finding and signing players.

sacrifice bunt

A bunt that a fielder fields for an out, but that results in a baserunner advancing.

sacrifice fly

A fly ball that a fielder catches for an out, but that results in a baserunner scoring.

save

When a relief pitcher comes into a close game and preserves a win.

utilityman

A member of a baseball team who plays various positions.

veteran

A player who has played many years.

walk-off

Any victory in which the home team scores the winning run in the bottom of the final inning.

MORE INFORMATION

BOOKS

Flynn, Brendan. *The MLB Encyclopedia*. Minneapolis, MN: Abdo Publishing, 2022.

Gitlin, Marty. *Baseball: Underdog Stories*. Minneapolis, MN: Abdo Publishing, 2019.

Hewson, Anthony K. *GOATs of Baseball*. Minneapolis, MN: Abdo Publishing, 2022.

ONLINE RESOURCES

To learn more about the New York Mets, please visit **abdobooklinks.com** or scan this QR code. These links are routinely monitored and updated to provide the most current information available.

INDEX

ABOUT THE AUTHOR

David J. Clarke is a freelance writer. Originally from Helena, Montana, he now lives in Savannah, Georgia, with his golden retriever, Gus.